Aug. 26, 1992

Dear Dori,

Happy Birthday!

Once again I want to remind
you that you are an
inspiration to me. I love
your charm, humor, and
brilliance.

I'll love you always.

Sarah

D1509342

PIERO
DELLA FRANCESCA

© 1991 Anaya Editoriale s.r.l./Fenice 2000 s.r.l., Milan
All rights reserved. No reproduction of this book in whole or in
part or in any form may be made without written authorization of
the copyright owner.
Created and produced by Fenice 2000 s.r.l., Milan, Italy
Text by Eleonora Bairati
Editorial direction by Lorenzo Camusso
Edited by Luca Selmi, Mady Rigoselli, Elizabeth Speroni
Picture research by Francesca Bonfante
Translation by Jay Hyams
Separations by Seby s.r.l., Milan
Typesetting by Fotocompograf s.r.l., Milan

This 1991 edition published by Crescent Books,
distributed by Outlet Book Company, Inc.,
a Random House Company
225 Park Avenue South, New York, New York 10003

ISBN 0-517-06133-3

Printed and bound in Italy

87654321

ELEONORA BAIRATI

PIERO
DELLA FRANCESCA

CRESCENT BOOKS
New York

CONTENTS

Images around Piero: landscapes, cities, and men

Florence, 1439. The city – prosperous, busy with commerce, the cradle of Renaissance civilization – is the scene of a memorable event: the ecumenical council called to reconcile the Eastern and Western churches has been transferred from Ferrara to Florence. For a short time, Florence becomes Europe's most cosmopolitan city.

Foreign delegations parade through the streets and squares, colorful Oriental costumes mixing with elegant Western dress. The expectancy and curiosity reach their peak with the arrival in the city of John VIII Palaeologus, Eastern emperor. Among the crowd that throngs to catch a glimpse of the great personage there is, perhaps, a young "foreign" artist, a provincial from an out-of-the-way town in the upper Tiber valley: Piero de' Franceschi, known – for reasons long lost – as Piero della Francesca. Even many years after that date, the unmistakable profile of Palaeologus, with the characteristic "little white hat pointed in front" – as recorded a chronicler of the period – as well as the people in strange Oriental costumes appear in Piero's works and bear witness to the force with which the visual memory of the event was impressed on his mind.

We know that in that same year of 1439 "Pietro di Benedetto del Borgo a San Sepolcro" worked in Florence with another "outside" artist, Domenico Veneziano, on the frescoes of the choir of the church of Sant'Egidio: this is the first certain record we have of Piero. As we will see, Piero's presence in Florence is an important fact for reconstructing his artistic career, but it is also an extremely elusive fact: we do not know how long he stayed in Florence; we do not know the style in which he then painted, since the frescoes of Sant'Egidio were later destroyed; we know nothing of the places he frequented or the people he knew, even if we can make reasonably good guesses. Florence immediately disappears from the horizon of Piero's existence (as far as is known, he never went back), nor does the artistic environment of Florence seem to show signs of his presence.

To find Piero we must look back to the place where he was born, Borgo San Sepolcro (today Sansepolcro, in the province of Arezzo), and from the image of a youth with eyes opened wide on the history and art of his time pass onto another, more pathetic image. A local chronicle from the 16th century records that a certain Marco di Longaro, a maker of "lanterns to be carried about," "when he was small, he led by hand master Piero di la Francesca, excellent painter, who had become blind." This moving image of the old, blind artist, great like King Lear or Homer, accompanied by his young guide, introduces us to the environment in which Piero spent most of his life: the alleys, narrow squares, modest buildings, and churches of Borgo, a place still today marked by that civilized and intact dimension so typical of the fabric of small Tuscan centers. Almost all of the scarce documentation that we have concerning Piero relates to his presence in Borgo.

He was born there, most probably around 1420, the first child of Benedetto de' Franceschi, shoemaker and tanner, and Romana di Perino da Monterchi. It was there that he obtained his first commissions. He always returned there from his travels as an apprentice and for work, living in Borgo as a respected and honored citizen – even if, in 1471, he forgot to pay his taxes and was registered as a debtor – and he there bought land, wisely administered his goods and those of his family, and occupied public offices (he served on the town council and was head of the priors of the Confraternity of San Bartolomeo). Piero spent all of the last period of his life in Borgo, in a quiet retirement not without intellectual activity: although he no longer painted because of the progressive weakening of his eyesight, he busied himself dictating his texts and treatises. On July 5, 1487, still "healthy in mind and body," he drew up his will, in which, aside from his heirs, he makes bequests to churches and confraternities of Borgo, arranging for his burial in the family tomb at Badia (now the cathedral of Sansepolcro). He died on October 12, 1492, by curious coincidence the very same day on which Christopher Columbus first touched the unknown lands of the New World, thus beginning – according to the traditional divisions of history – the modern age. Piero's life would by this classification belong to the Middle Ages. But historical periods do not always coincide with those of art: 15th-century artists were well ahead of the men of letters, the politicians, and the scientists. They were, and felt themselves to be, the initiators of a new age – the Renaissance – and it is in their efforts and achievements, more than in any other cultural aspect of the period, that can be found the foundations of the modern world.

A portrait conserved in Sansepolcro's civic museum and originally from the family of Marini Franceschi – even though late (from the end of the 16th century) and obviously ennobled for the greater glory of the family's descendents – gives us a certain approximation of the impressive character and face of Piero: a robust face, with the clear signs of energy. This same face can be found in an engraving published in the *Lives* of Giorgio Vasari (1568) and – with a greater margin of doubt – can perhaps be identified with two figures, assumed self-portraits, in the *Madonna of Mercy* and the *Resurrection of Christ*, two works of great prestige carried out for Borgo San Sepolcro. The fact that both these faces are foreshortened makes one almost see them as wilful "signatures" of the great "poet of perspective."

In Via Aggiunti in Sansepolcro, opposite the church of San Francesco, is Piero's home, which passed from his family to other ownership: a small building of pleasing 15th-century style that until the beginning of our century had a room on the second floor with frescoes, including the figure of Hercules today in Boston's Gardner Museum.

Piero's ties to the city and places of his birth were uninterrupted and deep, and clear traces of them can be found in his works. In the few signed works (four in all), his name is always followed by "de Burgo" or "de Burgo Sancti Sepulcri." The characteristic outline of the city, enclosed within walls with high towers and soaring church belltowers, appears in the background of his paintings beginning with his earliest works, such as the *Baptism of Christ* in London and the *St. Jerome* in Venice, to the latest, such as the *Nativity* in London. The landscape of the upper Tiber valley, with its crystalline river flowing in slow bends amid gentle hills, under a bright clear sky, can be recognized behind the sacred act in the *Baptism*, around the solitary meditation in the *St. Jerome* in Berlin, and as the background of the historic event of the battle of Constantine the Great in the fresco cycle he carried out in the church of San Francesco in Arezzo. Of course, these homages Piero constantly paid to his home turf must not be viewed as though they were the work of 19th-century landscape painters, seeking in them documentary realities as though they were photographs, or even the emotional reflection of the artist: they are mental landscapes, places from memory, both abstract and yet recognizable.

All of Piero's itineraries, both existential and artistic, began in Borgo. Only 38 kilometers separate Sansepolcro from Arezzo, where Piero left his greatest masterpiece, the fresco cycle in the choir of the church of San Francesco. A short distance from Sansepolcro is Monterchi, birthplace of Piero's mother; the graveyard chapel in that town has the splendid fresco of the *Madonna del Parto* – "Pregnant Madonna." From Sansepolcro, in the bottom of the valley, spread out the uneven and picturesque roads of the Apennine passes, still today intact in landscapes of rough beauty: to Bocca Trabaria, through the valley of the Metauro, toward Urbino; across the Viamaggio pass down through the lonely Val Marecchia all the way to the sea at Rimini. These are fundamental stops along Piero's itineraries. He also visited the great centers of the Italian Renaissance: aside from Florence, Ferrara and Rome; but due to some strange fate, none of these cities, like Florence, preserves any trace of his passing, if one excludes the much discussed and badly conserved fresco with St. Luke in the basilica of Santa Maria Maggiore in Rome.

Piero's world is geographically a secret world, and even today the visitor must discover and conquer it as though performing a pilgrimage: it is an ideal "province" of uncertain borders, between Tuscany, the Marches, and Romagna, closed on every side by the blue walls of mountains; a landscape that is severe but lovingly worked by the hand of man; towns, castles, and cities made man-sized. Against this background, along these roads, in this space, we must imagine the men Piero met during his life: the artists and the intellectuals he encountered in his research; the patrons, the men who believed in him and trusted to his art imperishable memories and glories.

First among these were the citizens of Borgo: artisans, merchants, farmers. There were the members of the Brotherhood of Mercy – Misericordia – whose portraits Piero painted kneeling under the great protective mantle of the Virgin, in the polyptych they commissioned. There were the cultured abbots of the Camaldolese abbey of St. John the

Baptist who ordered the *Baptism of Christ* now in London. There was Angiolo di Giovanni di Simone who, together with the friars of Sant'Agostino, paid for the polyptych destined for the altar of their church. There was Ludovico Acciaioli, captain of Borgo for the Florentine government and first gonfalonier of justice, who in 1460 asked for the Palazzo Pretorio a devotional fresco with his patron saint. There were the conservators of the commune of Borgo, who had a wall of the building that was their headquarters frescoed like a great public ex-voto with the *Resurrection of Christ*, the image-symbol found on the city's coat of arms. The small civic museum of Sansepolcro, located in the town hall, holds three certain works by Piero – two of which fundamental for his catalog – and one attributed to him: none of the world's greatest museums can boast as many. And of the small number of works by Piero – often only fragments – present in Italian and foreign museums, at least ten came originally from Sansepolcro, including the *Nativity*, now in London, which was bequeathed to the descendents of the painter.

The patronage of Borgo, for the most part religious, was routine and had traditional needs: the contract for the *Polyptych of Mercy* (1445) established in detail, as was the custom during the Middle Ages, the quality of the materials (the fine gold for the background, the ultramarine blue among the colors), the deadline for the work (within three years), and the total to be done by Piero himself (a mark of esteem, perhaps, but also related to the amount of payment established). As a serious "professional," as we would say today, Piero knew how to balance both the needs of his patrons and his own: he respected certain bonds, such as the archaic gold background, but neither the period of the deadline (the payment registered in 1462 was most probably the final payment) nor the amount of work he himself performed, since the participation of helpers on the lesser parts of the work is clear. Piero behaved in much the same way for another work for Borgo, the *Polyptych of St. Augustine*, commissioned in terms very similar to those just described in 1454, with a requested delivery within eight years: the final payment was made in 1469. Piero must have worked slowly – his technique is precise and meticulous – but nothing impeded him from completing his tasks: it is thought that in the period of time it took him to finish the two polyptychs he also carried out the work on the cycle of frescoes in Arezzo, which, because of their challenge and complexity, must have taken up most of his time (not to mention other possible travels and lesser works).

In another case – that of the polyptych for the convent of St. Anthony in Perugia – Piero's behavior was even more easygoing and not only because of the intervention of collaborators: the anomalous structure of the work, which has led to contrasting opinions among scholars, seems to be the result of a compromise accepted by the artist to satisfy his patrons and probably to end a work that was stretching on too long. This consisted of the assembly of two parts – the polyptych and the cyma – of differing conceptions.

Aside from any stylistic results – which in Piero never showed variations – secular patrons allowed him greater liberty and more adhesion to the major themes of his culture and his conception of art than did the local sphere of religious brotherhoods and orders. The great cycle in Arezzo is an important example of how positive such relationships could be. Since 1416 the Bacci, a wealthy family of Arezzo spice merchants, had had the patronage of the choir chapel of the church of San Francesco. Francesco Bacci began the fresco decoration of this chapel in 1447 by hiring Bicci di Lorenzo, an aging Florentine painter with a very traditional style. Francesco's oldest son, Giovanni, was a man of great culture and wide interests, with contacts in the humanistic sphere of Florence and Rome, where he performed the role of clerk to the Apostolic Chamber. We do not know if he was involved in the choice of Piero – who already enjoyed a certain fame in the area – to continue the work of Bicci, who died in 1452, but only a similar person would have made such an advanced choice to uphold the cultural ambitions of the family; and he may also have had some influence on the choice of the subjects, so new and special, of the cycle with the *Legend of the True Cross*, masterfully painted by Piero on the walls of the chapel. And it is also possible that Giovanni Bacci, with his intelligence and vast round of contacts, was responsible for other important commissions for Piero. At any rate, to this wealthy middle-class family and learned member goes the historical credit for supplying Piero with the opportunity to create his greatest work, the size and complexity of which – since the cycles of frescoes in Ferrara and Rome have been lost – cannot be compared to any other carried out for the most noble patrons.

The loss of works and absence of records do not permit us to judge Piero's relationships with Borso d'Este in Ferrara or with Pope Pius II in Rome, but sufficient documents exist on other important encounters, that illuminate how he developed his contacts with the leaders of his time and the position he held in the courtly environment. One should not fall into the trap of making the kind of facile sociological simplifications according to which Piero was a "courtly" artist: in his relationships with his powerful patrons he asserted – as did the other major artists of the time – the new dignity of the role of the artist, which had recently risen from the level of a mere artisan to that of an intellectual on an equal footing with men of letters and scientists.

The development of Italian Renaissance art is strictly tied to the culture of the wealthy courts that flourished not only in the larger cities but also in minor centers. The lords of these small states were usually military captains, audacious adventurers who had taken power with the force of arms and knew how to maintain it using intrigue or assassination. Although their dominions were often limited to a single city and never spread beyond the territory of a province, these rulers had the audacity to have themselves presented, on medallions and in portraits, like the Roman emperors who had conquered the world. Art and culture served to legitimize and ennoble their power: they surrounded themselves with poets and writers, sought out and collected precious manuscripts and ancient objects of art, enriched their cities with great buildings, competed among themselves – beyond their political rivalry – to obtain the services of the greatest artists of the moment, including architects, painters, sculptors, and decorators.

Men of this caliber were the great patrons of Piero: Sigismondo Pandolfo Malatesta, ruler of Rimini, and Federigo da Montefeltro, count and later duke of Urbino. Divided by a fierce rivalry and engaged in a struggle without quarter over a small expanse of territory – a struggle that ended with the ruin of the first and the victory of the second – they were united by an equal ambition to give their prestige to art and culture. They both made use of the same artists, and artists did not hesitate about offering their services to one or the other. The marks left by the two rulers on their respective cities were so decisive that they are still visible today. Rimini was only a small town until Sigismondo Malatesta imprinted on it the signs of his power and glory: the great towered complex of Castel Sismondo (1446) and the classical, marble mass of the Tempio Malatestiano (Malatesta Temple, 1450), designed by Leon Battista Alberti. Urbino was a small, picturesque medieval center on the side of a hill before Federigo II, with the creation of a great palace planned by Luciano Laurana, transformed it into the "city in the form of a palace" praised by Baldassar Castiglione. The fact that Piero was present in both of these cities during the most stimulating periods of their exultant growth is not an accident: he was, in fact, one of the determinant leaders of this growth in both cases.

Piero may have been sent to Rimini from Ferrara, where he worked during the years 1449 and 1450, given the ties between the Este and Malatesta courts (Ginevra d'Este was Sigismondo's first wife). A sort of migratory current of artists and workmen had been set up between Rimini and Urbino, making contacts between those two courts easy, and Piero probably began his contacts at the same time on both fronts around the middle of the century. The relationships the artist had with the two courts were at different levels, and the works he created – even when not supported by documents – clearly show this. In the case of Sigismondo, Piero seems to have been a follower, almost obsequious to the desires of his patron, and also personally detached; in the case of Federigo he seems more free to experiment but also a more intimate participant in the ideals of the patron. Such relationships also reflect the personalities of the two men involved.

A thread of cruelty winds through the life of Malatesta, "the stormy imperial soul/who had few castles and not the world" (D'Annunzio), as audacious and unscrupulous in his political dealings as he was learned and ambitious in his cultural moves. Even today one cannot read without emotion the classical dedicatory epigraph of the Malatesta Temple, written – not transliterated – in Greek, the first and only case in western Christianity. On the other hand one easily forgets that the temple was supposed to be a church: Pope Pius II (who excommunicated Sigismondo) was not completely wrong when he defined it "so full of pagan works that it seemed less a church than a temple for the heathen worshipers of the devil." The ruler's program of self-exaltation – including the fresco painted by Piero (1451) – is exhibited without the slightest restraint, and what might have been acceptable in a private home – there is the same thing in the ducal palace in Urbino, but in a more controlled way – was scandalous in a public building intended as a church.

No less audacious than Sigismondo as a *condottiere*, but far more shrewd politically and intelligent diplomatically, Federigo da Montefeltro knew how to confer on his lands the stable form of a state ruled by a wise "prince" legitimized by the prestige of culture and art. A refined connoisseur with sure taste, an expert in architecture, a humanist who succeeded in assembling one of the richest libraries of Greek and Latin texts (later given to the Vatican), in a dramatically short time Federigo brought Urbino to the level of the major Italian Renaissance centers, the privileged seat of what has been called "mathematical humanism" (Chastel), a melting pot of experiences open to foreign contributions, including those of Flemish and Spanish artists.

Piero's stay in Rimini, which coincided with the major work on the building of the Malatesta Temple, was probably not very long: the fresco in the temple and the portrait of Sigismondo now in the Louvre were both carried out at the same time. On the other hand, the artist visited Urbino several times and seems to have made long stays, given the quality and challenge of the works created: the *Flagellation of Christ*, the double portrait of Federigo and his wife, Battista Sforza, the altarpiece once the church of in San Bernardino and now in Milan's Brera, and, since it was probably for the same patron, the *Madonna of Senigallia*, span the time of the extraordinary development of Urbino's culture. Nor did Piero end his relationship with the court after his retirement to Sansepolcro: he dedicated his manual on perspective *De prospectiva pingendi* to Federigo, and to Federigo's son Guidobaldo he entrusted, with a moving dedication, his final work, composed in his "extreme age," the manuscript *De quinque corporibus regolaribus (On the Five Regular Bodies)*, asking him to place it in the great library his father had created, together with the other works of Piero that were assembled there.

If there is any place in this world, other than Sansepolcro, in which to seek out Piero, it must certainly be Urbino: in the proud and intact measure of the city on certain silent winter days, clear and windy; in the luminous spaces among the rooms in the ducal palace so evocative of refined intellectual encounters; in the light of the landscape of the valley of Foglia, which from Urbino descends toward Pesaro, the same light that saturates the background of water and hills in the portraits of the dukes of Montefeltro. In Urbino, Piero's art evolved more than in any other place, reaching new goals; in Urbino, Piero's work as a painter reached its conclusion; afterward there is only the sublime silence of geometry, the motionless radiation of the metaphysical harmony of regular bodies.

Images of Piero: the light of geometry

The language of Piero della Francesca represents both one of the highest achievements of the art of the Italian Renaissance and one of the most difficult keys to a full understanding of his importance. This seems to contradict the fact that Piero's style is so unique, so exclusively his own that it is recognizable on first sight and unmistakable with that of any other artist of his time (which explains why the compilation of the catalog of his works offered very few margins for error in attribution). Furthermore, it seems to contradict our own experience: before a painting by Piero we have a sense of fulfillment, everything seems clear, limpid, understandable; we are also, however, aware of a sense of distance, a kind of reverential detachment. The best metaphors for expressing this sensation are those of silence, quiet, immobility.

The great expert Bernard Berenson defined Piero's art as "ineloquent," a definition that seems perfect. There is no eloquence in a painting by Piero, no expressions of feelings or passions, events do not take place but are given; even in the most complex compositions, which for their very subjects seem irreconcilable with this principle – the great battles of the Arezzo cycle, for example – there is no drama, the leading characters are not disturbed by passion; gestures are not consequences of earlier gestures and do not signal later ones but are instead suspended in the instantaneousness of a fixed moment for all eternity.

Like all great painters, Piero communicates by way of elements strictly tied to visual language; one must learn these to understand the complexity of structure beneath those forms apparently so simple and natural, and to understand the extraordinary depth of meaning that is their substance. In art there is no meaning except that given in that single form. Understanding the art of Piero is thus like digging to the right depth to reach that sense of "intellectual certainty" (Focillon) that is the most rewarding experience of all.

Even for specialists and scholars, the reconstruction of the career of Piero is studded with doubts and difficulties: signed works are rare, and but few are dated or documented with any certainty; important sources have been lost, works have been violated, some have been dismembered and dispersed, others are in a poor state of preservation. There is also the disconcerting fact of a language that, from the first works, presents itself fully developed, already finished, and that evolves only through almost imperceptible adjustments, slow and thought-out deepenings, a coherent continuation without breaks. Establishment of a convincing chronology of Piero's works on the basis of style, in the absence of external elements to check or compare the works with, is thus very difficult.

To clarify the discussion and to fix indispensable reference points for a survey of Piero della Francesca's works, one can adopt a division into three principal phases: the first includes the works that precede the Malatesta Temple of Rimini (1451); the second groups together the works contemporary to the fresco cycle in Arezzo (1452-c. 1465); the third relates to the last period of his activity, most of all the work he carried out for the court of Urbino.

We know nothing of his apprenticeship - probably carried out in his hometown - nor of his early formation before his stay in Florence. Even so his earliest works reveal without any doubt that his apprenticeship must have been determinant and thus, most probably, also long. It is thought to have taken place around 1439.

In that period Florence could offer a young artist in formation an exceptional breadth of rich and varied experiences. From the beginning of the century the city had been moving steadily toward becoming the unquestioned capital of the new humanistic art. Piero's quick yet meditative intelligence could grasp the most advanced points of the figurative avant-garde as well as the moderate and more traditional trends: from the rigorous research into perspective of Brunelleschi to the more heterodox works of Paolo Uccello; from the plastic forms and natural truths of Donatello and Masaccio to the poetic light and color of Masolino and Fra Angelico; from the Romanized classicism of Nanni di Banco to the elegance of Lorenzo Ghiberti; from the fluid linearism of Filippo Lippi to the constructive energy of Andrea del Castagno. For several years the first treatise meant to provide painters with a solid theoretical and scientific base for their works had been in circulation, the *Della pittura* (1436) by Leon Battista Alberti. The importance this famous intellectual had for Piero must have been great, beginning with their first meeting and renewed across time, since their careers continued to cross afterward, from Ferrara to Rimini, from Urbino to Rome. Alberti, sought by the courts and by the most cultured circles in Italy, could give Piero precious support for being introduced into those environments.

Because of the long time of its execution, the *Polyptych of Mercy* is an exemplary text for judging how Piero acquired, assimilated, and adapted to his own needs his Florentine experiences, exposing them to a rigorous selective scrutiny. Among the first parts to be laid down, the *Crucifixion* in the cyma seems to make explicit homage to that painted by Masaccio in the polyptych for the church of the Carmine (1426), most of all in the dramatic accent, rare in the works of Piero. Identifying the differences is not difficult, however: the gestures of the characters, in particular that of St. John, who comes forward impetuously, spreading his arms, do not serve so much to heighten the dramatic sense of the scene – as in Masaccio – as to indicate the spatial directions of the composition. The traditional gold ground, that in Masaccio serves as the background against which he makes the sculptural energy of the figures stand out, becomes with Piero a factor of reflection and diffusion of light, another element of spatial definition. The haloes around the sacred personages, usually drawn on the gold background around their heads, become in Piero foreshortened and mirrored disks, in which their heads are reflected. Even the chiaroscuro that defines the statuesque figure of St. Sebastian is derived from Masaccio; Florentine effects are visible even in the greater evidence of linear contours. In the central partition with the *Madonna of Mercy*, which probably constitutes the final phase of the work, the lines are absorbed in a process of formal abstraction characteristic of Piero's style. The Virgin's mantle is as wide and solemn as a cupola to protect the faithful, the circular gathering of whom suggests the ideal completion of a hemisphere. The composition is like a cupola structure seen in section, of which the supporting column is the Madonna crowned by the perfect ovoid of her head, like a small dome. It is a mathematical theorem, but the evocative image of the building – Mary is the symbol of the Church, the house of God and his believers – is so convincing, so real, that only after later reflection does one become aware of the incongruous and archaic element of hierarchial scale in the proportions, according to which the figures of the faithful are much smaller than that of the Virgin, as in medieval presentations of the theme.

This image is an apt example of the prodigious equilibrium with which Piero succeeded in composing apparently contrasting trends: a thin thread of secular, humanistic culture, with strong scientific interests, and a thicker thread of devotional culture, with deep roots in the popular imagery, of which the artist made use until the end to obtain the understanding and psychological adherence of the faithful spectators.

Thus, Piero did not only accept the typological tradition of polyptychs, but he used also the current repertory of iconographic themes, renewing them from within, in the structuring of the image as in the density of the meaning. His works made for religious patrons are thus important to the understanding of how he moved between the traditional and the innovative, bearing in mind that we are in a "provincial" environment in which the ornate and decorative late Gothic style was still widespread.

Unfortunately, the only one of Piero's polyptychs that has been preserved structurally intact, albeit anomalous, is a late one from Perugia, and the missing link between the *Polyptych of Mercy* and that of Perugia was the *Polyptych of St. Augustine*, which has been dismembered and largely lost. Even the juvenile work *The Baptism of Christ* – which, however, cannot predate the first parts of the *Polyptych of Mercy* – must not have originally stood alone, so much so that later (1460-65) it was inserted, perhaps to make up for a failure to fulfill a commission on the part of Piero, as the central partition in an ornate triptych painted by Matteo di Giovanni, a local painter with Senese training, which is to say with the decorative and coloristic taste that was most common in the area around Arezzo. The ideal recomposition of the work – a simple photomontage suffices for this – provokes a surprising effect: the *Baptism*, in a context as sumptuous as it is conventional, opens before our eyes a totally new pictorial world. Gone is the golden background, and the sacred event takes place in an open landscape – that of the upper Tiber valley around Sansepolcro – under a brilliantly clear sky. This first encounter of Piero with nature is not at all like that – invested with abundant details and distracting curiosities – of the artists of the international Gothic style, nor is it the rough, bare, and primitive landscape of Masaccio. Piero's landscape is real, in as much as it refers to visual and mental experience, excluding every "accident" that does not contribute to a superior harmony. The mirroring surface of the river reflects the images without deforming them; the clouds are symbols to contribute visual measure to the incommensurable, like the forms of the white pigeons suspended on folded wings over Christ's head.

Just as several portions of the *Polyptych of Mercy* are reminiscent of Masaccio, so too echoes of Florentines are to be found in this work: the tender modelling of Masolino, in place of the constructive chiaroscuro of Masaccio; the fresh spring colors of Fra Beato Angelico and Domenico Veneziano, but with an even greater luminosity. Piero's colors rarely blare out and are usually in fact rather low-toned, but they are luminous because they are drenched with light, a light purified of every contingency, absolutely white and uniformly spread, that does not strike the forms violently from without but is the very substance of their being as form-light-colors.

By 1450, the date of *The Penitent St. Jerome* of Berlin, not only had Piero's style been perfectly formed, but he had also achieved complete autonomy with respect to the most important reference points of the period. The totality and stupendous coherence of the works Piero created during the period in which he executed the Arezzo cycle allow for the chronological and complete identification of the components of that style.

It is in this period, beginning (not at all by chance) with the frescoes for the Malatesta Temple, that the influence of Alberti becomes clearer. The problem confronted in Alberti's *Della pittura* was simple and fundamental: the transfer to a flat pictorial surface of the facts of visual experience. For Alberti, this was a problem inherent in plane geometry, for which reason he insisted the painter must be an expert at geometry. Piero showed himself completely convinced of this. His treatises – most of all *De prospectiva pingendi* – represent the passage from the high theories of Alberti (whose text was not accompanied by any graphic aids) to the practice in the enunciation and demonstration of geometric theorems with the scope of pictorial representations. But one must not consider Piero a scientist or mathematician who was also a painter. He was first of all a painter: for him geometric rules were not tools to be used from without to correct or coldly alter a pictorial impulse; they were, instead, ingrained and innate in painting itself. Alberti's propositions were actualized in Piero's art only as they served the needs of painting, and not vice versa, with rigor and also with liberty. From this comes that extraordinary unity of intellectualism and naturalness, of abstraction and concreteness, that creates the greater fascination of Piero's art.

For Alberti, the plane of presentation is like an open window; for Piero there is the clear tendency to give compositions a form that inclines to the perfectly balanced form of the square, and the "window effect" is accentuated by the frequent presence of a painted architectural cornice. In the Rimini frescoes the cornice is like a door opened to suddenly reveal the scene. In the Sansepolcro *Resurrection* the parapet and architrave between the Corinthian columns create the effect of a large window thrown open on the landscape. Even where the original cornice has been lost, as in the case of the stupendous diptych of portraits of the rulers of Urbino, can we sense its intimate, necessary presence; and particularly in this work, in which the figures, in the near foreground, are seen against a landscaped background just as though they were in reality viewed in front of a windowframe.

This form of visual concreteness, a desire to rationally circumscribe the painted surface so as to justify the opening onto what is represented, brings us to reflect on the use Piero makes of the rules of perspective.

Perspective, experimentally invented by Brunelleschi and then codified by Alberti in the geometric process of what he called the *costruzione legittima* (scientifically correct construction), became a powerful tool for giving internal cohesion and coherence to the representation, instituting for the first time a direct relationship, scientifically foreseeable and calculable, between the representation and the spectator. But Renaissance perspective is much more than a technical expedient. It is, instead, a rational principle for measuring and understanding – and thus controlling – space as an area for the actions of men and history. In a period in which art and science were closely connected, the rationalization of vision offered by perspective expressed a radical turn in the way of thinking, in the very concept of man and history. For this reason, the invention of perspective around the beginning of the 15th century can be considered as important, if not more important, for the birth of the modern world as was the discovery of America with which that century ended.

For Piero della Francesca, the identification of perspective with painting was complete. We must be careful, however, to not fall into the error of believing that for him perspective signified the way of obtaining an illusionistic mimesis of natural reality. He never forgot the reality of the plane, and in his works perspective never "breaks," is not scenographic, does not seek to fool the eye with illusionistic effects: it is instead the rational principle for the organization of the represented space following internal rules that belong to art, not to nature. Precisely in Piero, the artist most intimately connected with Alberti's codification, we can discover how perspective was an agile and experimental tool, not at all rigid and academic, in the hands of gifted painters.

Perspective drawing of a Corinthian capital from Piero della Francesca's De prospectiva pingendi.

Alberti's "scientifically correct construction" was strongly centralized and perfectly symmetrical. Piero, on the other hand, never makes use of a central vanishing point toward which all the lines – the "orthogonals" – converge, nor does the vanishing point ever fall along the ideal central line of the composition. In the same way, Piero was not drawn to bilaterally symmetrical compositions, a consequence of a rigorously centralized organization, and shows instead a fondness for a harmonic relationship that is more complex and flexible, that of the golden section, broken down by a vertical component that falls near the median line, usually located to the right. This compositional method is already present in the *Baptism*, in which, this time on the left, the pale trunk of a tree divides the image in two parts. In the more complex and mature development of this spatial organization of paintings, the double division is carried out by architecture, the preferred form being an open loggia, one column of which constitutes the dividing element, usually joined to an architectural system that leads to the background of the painting. The first example of this articulation is found in the *Flagellation of Christ* of Urbino, in which the geometric partition – the opening of the loggia being almost a square – is particularly evident. This becomes a recurring theme in the Arezzo cycle; and we find it again, in a more ambiguous form, in the *Annunciation* in Perugia and the *Virgin and Child with Angels* in Williamstown.

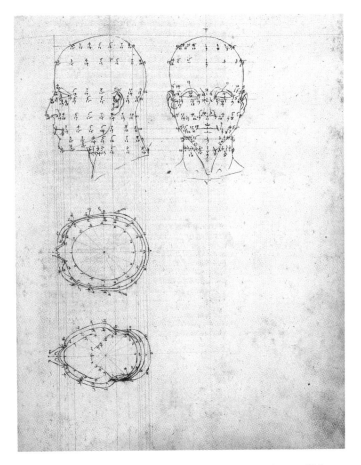

The human head as drawn in De prospectiva pingendi *by Piero della Francesca.*

All the visual elements lead back across the plane, regardless of their reciprocal distance, and since Piero has faith in the absolute value of geometry, he does not worry about correcting any visual ambiguities that the representation might involve. As for the diminishing of objects, we know that the landscape in the background of the *Baptism* is distant, but we cannot determine just how far away it is; indeed, we have the impression that it is closer than it should be, almost as though it were hung behind the figures. The Virgin in the *Annunciation* in Perugia seems to be in front of the open gallery, since her figure stands out against the dark background of the arcade, but in reality she is standing in the space between two columns. In the Brera altarpiece the figures seem to be aligned just in front of the apse and even partially within it, but perspectival reconstruction has demonstrated that they are actually a good distance in front of it. Looking at the large compositions of the battles in the Arezzo cycle, the first impression is of a giant puzzle of colored shapes and only after focusing on the work does one become aware of the masterful spatial hierarchy.

This fascinating mosaiclike effect, with forms and colors, a result of the geometrical reduction of forms on a plane, relates to the particular way Piero delineates and colors. The drawing, the primary element in Florentine art, is not used by Piero to define the individual forms taken one at a time, making them stand out with contour lines: the

lines instead disappear and become only an imperceptible border that circumscribes one portion of the surface, which comes alive in the relationship with the other contiguous portions by virtue of rhythmic and coloristic values. The most obvious symptom of this way of understanding painting can be identified in the unique process Longhi called the "principle of formal and chromatic inversion": figures or parts of figures are mirrored; colors are repeated and alternated like a chiasmus to create a sovereign equilibrium and a perfect harmony. In the frescoes of the Malatesta Temple we see two crouching greyhounds, one against the other, one light and one dark, as though they were a heraldic symbol; in the retinue of the Queen of Sheba in the Arezzo cycle the two grooms are almost the same figure, seen from in front and from behind, the colors of their clothes and stockings rhythmically inverted; and in the group of the queen's ladies, in two contiguous scenes, the same faces and profiles appear, turned to the right or to the left, obtained with the use of the same preparatory cartoon. The most outstanding example of the application of this principle is the *Madonna del Parto* in Monterchi, in which the figures of the two angels were created with the use of the same cartoon turned round and the colors of their clothes, stockings, and wings are symmetrically inverted. Although these might seem simple technical expedients, tricks of the trade, they do not indicate any lack of imagination on the part of Piero: they serve to accentuate the ceremonial or liturgical gravity of the image and are indications of a powerful desire for equilibrium, of a vision of the world *sub specie* of the absolute mathematical. Piero tends to conceive each form as the perfect measure of a regular solid, even those that, for their specific individuality, do not seem reducible to such a form – the human body, for example. Thus Piero's heads become perfect ovoids, long necks form cylinders; and there is the stupefying page of his *De prospectiva pingendi* in which a human head is sectioned like a geometrical solid to display its exact construction. Thus there is the architectural quality of his figures, made clear by the folds in their clothing that resemble the grooves of columns. In reality all of Piero's painting is intimately architectural for it tends toward the monumental and abstract qualities of architecture – a non-expressive, non-narrative art. It is more like music, and not by accident do musical terms, such as rhythm and pause, come to mind when seeking to define Piero's compositional methods.

The way in which all these characteristics, which might appear unrelated to every illustrative intention, can find full expression in a large work with a narrative content is best demonstrated by the Arezzo cycle. The *Legend of the True Cross*, with its fantastic mixture of myth, fable, and history, was a much-loved subject of the Franciscan order. Piero had behind him several illustrious Tuscan precedents, and he must certainly have been aware of the well grounded iconographic tradition.

Using the age-old story related in Jacopo da Varagine's *Golden Legend*, Piero selected the fundamental episodes, discarding some, emphasizing others, inserting some that had at times been neglected. The same liberty he took in the selection of the episodes he used in the organization of the narrative order. Having at his disposition two large walls and a narrow minor wall that joined them, interrupted by an ogival window, Piero adopted the traditional partition of 14th-century decorations of similar Gothic chapels, distributing the various scenes on superimposed registers. The logical sequence of the events does not correspond, however, to a linear and continuous reading of the frescoes. What primarily interested Piero was the internal, visual coherence of the cycle, so this is composed following a precise and preordained drama of rhythmic correspondences, of compositional symmetries and analogies of content and form.

Beginning from above, according to the operative routine that provided for a single scaffolding with the simultaneous work on the two walls, the two facing lunettes show the beginning and end of the story: the *Death of Adam* (to the right) and the *Return of the Cross to Jerusalem* (to the left), both scenes located in wide-open spaces. On the short wall are two figures of *Prophets*, heroes of the biblical world and prefigurations of the Christian world. On the lower register are two facing scenes of sacred and ceremonial subjects: the *Adoration of the Sacred Wood* and the *Meeting of Solomon and the Queen of Sheba* (to the right) and the *Finding of the Three Crosses and the Verification of the True Cross* (to the left), both divided in two episodes, of which one takes place in the open and the other in a constructed environment. On the short wall are two scenes that could be defined as showing daily life: the *Transportation of the Sacred Wood* (to the right) and the *Torment of the Hebrew Judas* (to the left), both in the environment - again with one scene in the open and the other in an urban setting - of the contiguous scenes on the large walls. On the lower register are shown two enormous battle scenes, both victories of Christianity: that of Constantine the Great over the pagan emperor Maxentius (to the right), and that of Heraclius over Cosroe (to the left), completed by the episode of the imminent decapitation of the defeated ruler. On the short wall are two miraculous announcements brought by angels: the *Annunciation* to the Virgin (to the left) and the *Dream of Constantine* (to the right). The presence of an Annunciation is completely anomalous to the cycle of the legend: Piero has synthesized all that happened from the incarnation of the Word to the death of Christ on the cross. It should be noted, however, that even the episode of the *Transportation of the Sacred Wood* in the upper register can be read as a prefiguration of the journey to Calvary, as shown by the diagonal position of the wood and the comportment of the carrier, whose head - in a wonderfully evocative optical effect - is encircled by the natural grain of the wood as though by a halo.

To follow the order of the events, the eye of the viewer would have to take a rather uneven course from one wall to the other; but no need to do so is sensed, and instead the viewer is taken in by the visual satisfaction of the spectacular unfolding of the scenes and by the great and pleasing chromatic luminosity. Only slowly does one enter the game of the rhythmical correspondences, be-

coming aware of the mirror order in the preferred binary reading of the scenes, and one becomes aware that the chromatic register of the frescoes is tightly controlled, almost parsimonious, but extraordinarily refined (one notes the incredible variety of white tones).

In spite of the presence of helpers - inevitable for an undertaking of this size - and of probable interruptions, the cycle appears compact, almost as though born whole in a single instant. But within the work are important changes that were made with the meditated continuity characteristic of Piero's working style. The lunette with the *Death of Adam*, with the beautiful series of nudes that marks the phases of primitive humanity, from adolescence to the decrepitude of old age, is almost an homage to Florentine culture, which was very interested in the study of human anatomy and imbued with classicism. But the classicism of these images has nothing to do with archaeology: it is the pure expression of the most ancient, mythical phase of human history, which continues to unfold, in events of great nobility, on the lower registers. Interest in the perspective structure of images and in architecture dominates the middle register. This architecture shows clear signs of Alberti's influence, not only because of the classicism of certain elements - perfectly proportioned columns and capitals - but also for its predilection for marbled mirrorings, which are both geometrical elements for modeling the space and planes for pictorial use.

The most important innovation for the future, and not only in the works of Piero, has to do with the use of light. In the *Dream of Constantine* we find ourselves facing the first nocturnal in the history of Italian painting, and it has a stupefying wealth of luminous effects: the natural clarity of the night sky is broken by the sudden flash of miraculous light emanating from the flying angel, light that illuminates the tent, emphasizes the whiteness of the sheets and the clothes inside the tent, and is reflected dazzlingly on the armor of the soldiers on guard. In the battle scenes in the lower register this skill in the use of the effects of light is displayed in the full glare of a noonday sun.

This wealth of internal developments in the cycle underlines its importance among Piero's works and, thanks to internal cohesion, helps to locate in time a nucleus of works, based on a relative chronology.

The *Flagellation* in Urbino can be placed between the frescoes in the Malatesta Temple in Rimini and the first phases of the Arezzo cycle. Looked at closely, this composition recalls the *Baptism of Christ* because of the similar presence of a group of three figures to the side of the sacred event; but here the new complexity of the spatial arrangement is underlined by the imposition in the foreground of personages on the right, while the scene of the flagellation is vertiginously thrown into the distance by the magisterial perspective created by the architecture of the portico. The space spread parallel to the pictorial plane in the Rimini fresco is here articulated in depth, and the supremacy of the architecture derived from it is such that it makes the small picture a kind of prototype, the experimental model for the monumental solutions of Arezzo: the

View of an Ideal City, *by an unknown 15th-century artist (Urbino, Galleria Nazionale delle Marche).*

open gallery that frames the meeting of Solomon and the Queen of Sheba, the portico of the *Annunciation*.

A small group of minor works seems formed by extrapolations, projections based on models from the Arezzo frescoes: the *St. Julian* of the museum of Sansepolcro is a twin brother of the prophet of Arezzo; the *Hercules* today in Boston is a young, giant version of the same mythical progeny of the descendents of Adam; the *Mary Magdalen* of the Arezzo Cathedral seems to have stepped out of the retinue of ladies of the Queen of Sheba, though a few more pictorial subtleties have been added, including a thread of light in her hair and a crystal ointment vase that is in truth a container for luminous reflections.

The solemn ceremonial atmosphere of certain scenes in the Arezzo cycle becomes absorbing ritual in the *Madonna del Parto* of Monterchi, a singular image in Italian sacred iconography: with an identical, simultaneous gesture, two angels pull back the sides of a pavilion tent – similar to that in which Constantine received his dream – to reveal the figure, at the same time sacred and movingly human, of the pregnant Virgin. The aristocratically elegant gesture of one of the women of the retinue of the Queen of Sheba is here transformed into the Madonna's way, so true and touching, of resting an overturned hand on the thigh to help bear the weight of the baby.

The experiments with light found in the final phase of the Arezzo cycle show up in the *Resurrection* of Sansepolcro, subtly waning in the growing luminosity of a landscape at dawn, a triumphant light that strikes the body of Christ and is reflected off the soldiers in the foreground. The sense of supreme domination of the statuesque figure of Christ is created with an ingenious, striking difference in perspective, that makes use of two different points of view, in a way that moves from the strong foreshortening of the soldiers to the stately presence of the Redeemer.

The wealth of this creativity, carried out during the period of just over a decade, would not seem to leave room for further innovations, but the last period of Piero's activity presents precisely those innovations. If one can speak of an evolution in his always coherent style, this was the moment not for a change but for further developments on the base of the already obtained results toward experimentation, toward new goals. Without doubt this drive toward new areas was stimulated by Piero's experiences at the Urbino court, scene of a lively intellec-

tuality. The fervor that the great sponsor Federigo da Montefeltro was able to bring to the construction of the ducal palace represented for Piero an ideal environment. The themes on which he concentrated his attention were principally a new exploration of the relationship between figures and space, between painted architecture and real space, between the represented space and the space of sensible experience; the research, increasingly subtle, into the values and qualities of light; and finally a greater attention to the infinite richness of nature. All together, this was a route that went from the supremacy of architecture and perspective to the supremacy of painting.

Standing as an emblem at the beginning of this route is the *Flagellation*. The ideal relationship that ties the painted architecture of the picture to the real architecture of the palace of Urbino is so apt – entering the courtyard of honor of the palace one has the impression of entering the gallery of the *Flagellation* – that it can be taken as an important indication of the supervision of the "mathematical" minds of Piero and Alberti over the plan masterfully realized by Luciano Laurana. We should remember that Leon Battista Alberti dedicated to Federigo da Montefeltro his treatise on architecture (*De re aedificatoria*) and that the Urbino culture, more than any other, reveals that desire to coordinate every aspect of art to the unifying authority of architecture, the dominant theme of the second half of the 15th century. No image better expresses this climate than the celebrated architectural perspective painting known as the "ideal city," preserved in Urbino, for which – and not without good arguments – the hand of Piero has been often proposed. But even if the work is not a result of his hand, it clearly expresses his thoughts as put forth in the complex articulation of the *Annunciation* in Perugia. Like the *Flagellation*, this work belongs to that taste for painted architecture especially cultivated in Urbino and later expanded during the last decades of the century throughout the whole of central Italy.

In the same polyptych in Perugia we find different accents, unusual luministic fineness in the reduced spaces and in the small scenes of the platform. Up to this work, Piero's solemn and monumental art had not bent to gather the poetry of the minimal, of the smallest things: looking now at the *St. Augustine* of the dismembered polyptych for Sansepolcro, one notes the extreme optical fineness, almost miming the technique of embroidery, with which are painted the stories of the saint's sumptuous cape and mitre, and that thread of light that so clearly defines the crystal staff of the crosier. These innovations, also, are the result of the climate of Urbino.

From the period of his stay in Ferrara, Piero must have been aware of Flemish art and may even have encountered the great Roger van der Weyden in that very city. In Urbino this awareness must have been increased not only because of the presence there of Flemish works in the collection of the Montefeltros, but because of the activity of "northern" artists in the region of the Marches, including the Fleming Joos van Ghent and the Spaniard Pedro Berruguete. That Piero was affected by this contact is doubtless, as doubtless as the distance that separated his world of painting from that of the Flemings. Piero never shows that kind of hierarchial indifference shown by the Flemings, for which a face, a curtain, or a flower all have the same value. Nor does he share that uninterrupted – and fascinating – swarm of details, for he never abandoned the supreme control of an intellectual order that governs in a classical equilibrium the world of painting.

Proof of this is a stupendous courtly and ceremonial work with a purely "courtly" content: the diptych with the portraits of Federigo da Montefeltro and of his wife, Battista Sforza, with allegorical triumphs of the two rulers on the back. From the immediate nearness of the faces to the indefinite distance of the background landscape, the eye of Piero investigates every wrinkle, every strand of hair, every pearl in the jewels or embroidery of the clothes, and thus even every slope of a hill or bend of a river all the way to the blue horizon. To the concrete historical reality of the two figures - Federigo in the humanistic dress, Battista in the precious, jeweled dress of court - is joined the abstract quality of solid geometry – the cylinder, the sphere - and by way of subtle, luminous transitions the profiles "turn" in the atmosphere, suggesting the complete symmetry of the image. We should not forget the secular and worldly character of this work, nor its function as a eulogy for the dynasty.

We must now look at two religious works - the Madonna known as the *Madonna of Senigallia*, and the *Nativity* now in London. The first is without doubt of Flemish derivation, with its setting in a domestic interior: to the left one notes the wonderful effect of sunlight entering through a leaded-glass window and projecting its golden motes into the background; and to the right, on a platform in a niche, a small still life in a wicker basket with white linen. The space of this silent interior, so reminiscent of the rooms of the ducal palace of Urbino, is dominated by the solemn figure of the Virgin who holds the blessing baby, as robust as a little Hercules and as absorbed as the two angels by his side. The entire painting is a harmonious blend of pink, gray, and white, with golden strands in the hair and slight glints of pearl. In the *Nativity*, in a context very near the Flemish even in certain iconographic motifs - the nude baby laid on the ground on the edge of the Virgin's cloak – central importance is given to the classic concert of musician angels, which resemble the Florentine choir of Luca della Robbia. Notwithstanding the poor condition of

the work, we can still appreciate the pictorial skill of each detail: the landscape, the view of Sansepolcro, the shadows and the light of the hut, the braying ass, the rustic St. Joseph seated on the ass's saddle.

The touching intimacy of this work should not lead us to suppose a sort of withdrawal on the part of Piero with respect to the "minor" themes of his last period of activity, which instead brings us to the presence of his most innovative work, that most dense with importance for the entire future of Italian painting: the votive painting once in the church of San Bernardino in Urbino and now in the Brera Academy in Milan, the last work Piero carried out for Federigo da Montefeltro.

The painting takes up again the iconographical theme proposed in several works by Beato Angelico around 1440, of the "sacred conversation," a colloquy on doctrinal themes that is imagined to have taken place among a group of saints in the presence of the Virgin and Child. In Piero's work, for the first time, the conversation takes place within a churchlike building with clear and monumental Alberti-like forms: the relationship between the architecture and the solemn group of figures is close and of great visual complexity, since all attention, including that of the spectator, is drawn into it. The architectural outlines on the sides suggest the continuation of the architectural structure beyond the limits of the painting, into an open spatiality completely new and accentuated by an unusual variety of richness in the sense of sources of light. Light shines on every moulding or detail of the architecture, draws reflections from the jewels of the angels, from the crystal cross of St. Francis, from the embossings on the book of St. Andrew, and achieves its maximum optical shine off the armor of Federigo, kneeling in the foreground, in which is reflected a window that is not visible in the painting. The masterful use of perspective, the spatial experimentation, and the poetic use of light and pictorial grace make this the most extraordinary testament of Piero's works, and no other of his works had so great an effect on the future. In this phase, in the context of the environment of Urbino, the singular art of Piero is joined to the lively experience that the work itself urges and that prepares for the determinant change at the end of the century. It was there, in Urbino, that Piero's art turned into a kind of school, becoming the necessary formative base for the artists later defined as being his "creations": Melozzo da Forlì, Luca Signorelli, Donato Bramante; across more subtle ways Pietro Perugino; and by way of an almost genetic descendence in the climate of Urbino, the genius for new times, Raphael. But the last phase of Piero's work served to fecundate another context: across routes that are difficult to define but nonetheless certain, the most Flemish of all the Italian artists, Antonello da Messina, came in contact with it during his memorable leap from the south to the north of Italy. After just a few years, the altarpiece Antonello made for the church of San Cassiano in Venice transferred to Veneto the innovations of the altarpiece now in Brera; and Giovanni Bellini, who also at the same time was aware of the art of Piero, was able to draw from it the consequences of extraordinary

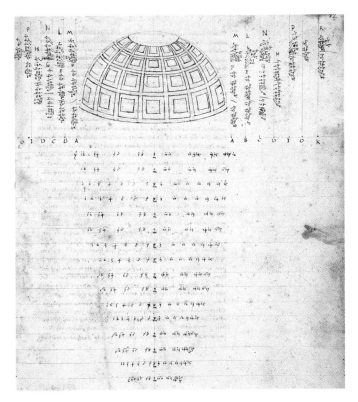

Drawing of an apse from De prospectiva pingendi *by Piero della Francesca.*

importance that led to a new course for Venetian art. Thus, as had already happened during the 14th century with Giotto, the art of a "provincial" painter, in this case from Borgo San Sepolcro, took on the role of a unifying experience, ultraregional, opening the way for a "national" language of art that became the shining merit of the great artists of the later Renaissance.

Even when we have mastered all the components of Piero's language, when we have entered into a confidential rapport with the complex and subtle themes of the relationships that support his compositions, there still remains yet one more path that must be followed to understand, going beyond the evidence of the images, the wealth of meaning that they contain.

Let us take a very simple composition, such as that of the fresco in the Malatesta Temple. The iconographic theme is one from the medieval tradition: the patron has wanted himself portrayed in the act of paying devotional homage to his patron saint. There is not, however, any hierarchical difference between the two figures, nor any sign of transcendence: the scene takes place in the room of a palace, almost as though it were the solemn reception given an ambassador. The saintly king of Bohemia holds the traditional attributes of his rank, the scepter and the globe, but his face – with a modern headcovering that gives it the character of a portrait – is the historic face of the emperor Sigismond of Luxembourg, who in 1433 had conferred on the youthful Malatesta the investiture of knight. This act not only legitimized the nobility of Sigismondo – an illegitimate son – but could easily be read as a favorable boon to his future good fortune.

To the right of the composition, in the marbled mirror of the walls, opens, with surprising visual effect, a small window through which can be seen a castle: as explained by the writing beneath the window, this is Castel Sismondo, completed in 1446. Bearing in mind that this work is in the Malatesta Temple, the image synthesizes the most evident and noble signs of the rule of Sigismondo over Rimini. The use of ancient iconography thus transforms the devotional theme into a secular one, marked by the courtly and solemn tone of a court ceremony that exalts the ruler, all undertaken with subtle and allusive discretion.

On another level, less clearly stated but of even greater meaning, is the use of legendary or historical facts in the Arezzo cycle, a use that reveals the thematic decisions made by Piero. For example, what is the significance of the emphasis put on the episode of the meeting between Solomon and the Queen of Sheba, an event that the other cycles of the legend do not include? And why are there two battles that seem to be replicas of each other, another element ignored by Piero's predecessors?

To answer these questions we must go back to the political climate of the historical moment in which Piero found himself and in which he worked. We have already made reference to the council held in 1439 to reconcile the Eastern and Western churches, an occurrence that had not just a theological and doctrinal importance but also a clear political weight since it included the appeal for the union of Christianity against the advance of the heathen Turks. The encounter between Solomon – the great king of the house of David, from whom Christ was to descend – and the Queen of the fabulous lands of the Orient, in the gesture of a handshake, is an expression of concord and allegiance and can be interpreted as a reevocation of the solemn concilar assizes of the two churches and as a hope for a harmonious meeting between the West and the East, united in a common faith. This union became even more necessary after 1453, when the Turks occupied Constantinople: the fall of the age-old capital of the Eastern Empire, the "second Rome," had such a large impact on Italy that Pope Pius II, in 1459, held a council at Mantua to call for a holy crusade to liberate the city; and the greatest hopes for a redemption of humiliated Christianity were hidden in the emperor John VIII Palaeologus. In the light of these events, one can understand why the patrons of Piero – Giovanni Bacci first in line – suggested the possibility of attributing to the episodes of this legend political and propagandistic functions related to the present, a suggestion that the artist took and carried out with the complete independence of his creative abilities.

It was not by accident that the members of the Bacci family had themselves portrayed among the group that witnesses the scene of the condemnation of the heathen king Cosroe, defeated by the emperor Heraclius. And we understand now why in the great scene of the battle of Milvian Bridge Constantine, the first Christian emperor, bears the traits of John VIII Palaeologus; and how the tie that joins in historical sequence the two battles projects itself into the hopes and fears of the contemporary world, expressing the faithful hope in a new, inevitable victory of Christian civilization, a never-forgotten component in the new secular civilization of humanism.

The convincing proof of this reading of the work is in a certain sense projected into that of another work, the *Baptism of Christ*, which illuminates meanings invisible to a first glance. The iconography of the painting is usual for an evangelical event, but the angels, to the left, do not hold, as tradition would have it, the vestments of Christ or the white linens of the baptism ritual. Indeed, they do not even seem to be witnessing or participating in the event. The three luminous young figures are connected to one another like a sculptural group, and the gestures of the handshake and the pat on the back have been interpreted, on the basis of ancient sources, as symbols of the theme of concord. If we then notice that in the background of the scene appears a group of dignitaries in Oriental costume, we might think that we find ourselves in the presence of another allusion to the council of 1439. The patronage of the work might even support such a hypothesis, given the objective of the Camaldolite order in the reconciliation of the church.

Even when Piero seems to be faithfully following the traditional iconography of a sacred subject, it is not rare to encounter an unexpected richness of additional meanings. It is thus with the *Resurrection of Christ* in Sansepolcro. According to an ancient legend, the foundation of Borgo was the work of two pilgrim saints who set up on the spot an oratory in memory of their visit to the Holy Sepulchre (Santo Sepolcro in Italian) in Jerusalem. The sacred image thus takes on also a certain civic value, underlined by the work's patronage and location. But there is even more: if we look at the background landscape with attention, we note that to the left the hills are bare and the trees without leaves, while to the right the land is fecund with cultivations and bushy trees. The resurrection of Christ is thus also a symbol of the rebirth of nature, of its perpetual renovation in spring after the death of winter. We must remember that the civilization of the birthplace of Piero was still deeply tied to the peasant's world, to a culture with a millenary tradition that made reference to the most ancient beliefs connected with the unchangeable rhythms of the seasons and agricultural labors. And the agricultural-pastoral world of the upper Tiber valley, as with all strongly conservative cultures, held deep traces of the survival of ancient rites and pre-Christian myths.

The *Madonna del Parto* of Monterchi – whose presence in that area would seem surprising – is a very evocative example of this. The small church that preserves the fresco was only later adapted to serve as a cemetery chapel and was at that time a small Marian sanctuary isolated in the countryside. The work certainly has a eucharistic meaning: Mary is the living tabernacle that encloses the invisible presence of the incarnate Word. In 15th-century Italian sculpture it is not rare to come upon tabernacles crowned by a tent held open by two angels. Recent research has, however, revealed the presence, in all the area of Monterchi and particularly in the area of the small church, of traces of ancient cults connected to feminine divinities that bring fecundity to the world of nature and are protectors of childbirth. The uninterrupted and lively devotion of women in the area to the image – the reason, perhaps the primary one, for its preservation in spite of many difficulties – is thus tied to a tradition that extends far into pre-Christian times.

Mere suggestions? Chance coincidences? A work of art always bears within itself the potential for various meanings, and each interpretation will appear more or less apt according to how well it seems to suit the image. This can be seen in relationship to certain writings, the results of recent trends in iconographical interpretation, that often force the limits that should be maintained to remain within the sphere of correctness and likelihood, out of respect for the intentions of the artist and the historical reality of the work itself.

Among the most discussed works are naturally those born in the cultured realm of the Urbino court. The Brera altarpiece has been carefully analyzed, particularly the complex relationships that tie the religious and liturgical meanings to the images of dynastic meanings, all in relationship to the patronage. The symbolic ostrich egg that hangs in midair in the vault of the apse – on the significance of which rivers of ink have been poured – can be taken as a symbol, according to a medieval tradition, of the miraculous incarnation, but it is also a heraldic symbol of the Montefeltros. The undoubted votive value of the altarpiece, with the patron kneeling in the foreground, can be broken down along various levels of meaning, from the personal to the political, alluding to the much-anticipated birth of an heir to the death of the mother of Battista on one side, to the military victories of Federigo and the exaltation of his power, made legitimate and almost sacred by the act of humble homage in the presence of the divine, on the other.

Interpretative research has reached unusual heights in relationship to the most enigmatic work of Piero, the *Flagellation of Christ*. Without doubt the true "subject" of the work relates to the group of figures in the foreground to the right, and the sacred scene is an evocation tied by an intrinsic but unreachable relationship with the three people and their silent conversation. But none of the readings seeking to clarify the sense of that relationship is really convincing, and some are obviously deviant. Nor can any of the three people be identified with any certainty. But even the earliest testimonies concerning the work place it in relationship with the events of the Montefeltro family: it was the desire of the patron to make the character of the work cryptic, and its reduced size confirms that it was intended for private use. And here we must stop, in the absence of valid and documented facts concerning its commission, its original location, or even the date of its creation. We must stop out of respect for the work itself, stop our search with humility in the face of the "resistence" that the work presents our interpretative analysis and consider ourselves rewarded by its richness, made even greater by the ambiguity of its meaning. On the other hand, as Ernst Gombrich justly put it, "The intensity of an artistic experience does not necessarily coincide with any clarity of understanding."

Works

1. *Polyptych of Mercy, 1445-62; Sansepolcro, Museo Civico; 273 x 323 cm entire; tempera on wood*
Commissioned by the Brotherhood of Mercy (Misericordia) for its church in Sansepolcro in 1445,
the work went ahead slowly over the course of more than fifteen years. The small figures of saints
on the side columns and the scenes from the life of Christ on the predella are not by Piero.

2. Polyptych of Mercy: The Crucifixion; *81 x 52.5 cm*

3. Polyptych of Mercy: The Crucifixion; *detail*

4. Polyptych of Mercy: St. Benedict of Norcia *(left); 54 x 21 cm;*
Angel of Annunciation *(right); 55 x 20.5 cm; partitions from the upper register to the left*

5. Polyptych of Mercy: The Virgin of the Annunciation (left); 54 x 21 cm;
St. Francis of Assisi (right); 54.5 x 21 cm; partitions from the upper register to the right

6. Polyptych of Mercy: St. Sebastian and St. John the Baptist; *each 109 x 45 cm;*
lateral partitions to the left

7. Polyptych of Mercy: St. Andrew and St. Bernardine of Siena; *each 109 x 45 cm;*
lateral partitions to the right

8. Polyptych of Mercy: The Madonna of Mercy; *134 x 91 cm; central partition*

9. Polyptych of Mercy: The Madonna of Mercy; detail

29

10. The Flagellation of Christ, *1450-55; Urbino,*
Galleria Nazionale delle Marche; 58.4 x 81.5 cm; wood
Signed "OPUS PETRI DE BURGO SCI SEPULCRI"

11. The Baptism of Christ, c. 1448-50; London, National Gallery; 166 x 115 cm; tempera on wood
Probably made for the altar of St. John the Baptist in the Camaldolite abbey of Sansepolcro (which later
became a cathedral), the picture was adapted to serve as the central partition of a triptych done by the
Senese painter Matteo di Giovanni around 1460-65, today preserved in the Museo Civico of Sansepolcro.

12. The Baptism of Christ; *detail*

13. St. Jerome and a Devout, c. 1450; Venice, Galleria dell'Accademia; 49 x 42 cm; tempera on wood
Signed "PETRI DE BU(R)GO S(AN)C(T)I SEP/ULCRI OPUS"

14.The Penitent St. Jerome, 1450; Berlin-Dahlem, Gemäldegalerie; 51.5 x 38 cm; tempera on wood
Signed and dated "Petri de Burgo opus MCCCCL"

15. Portrait of Sigismondo Pandolfo Malatesta, *1450-51; Paris, Musée du Louvre; 44.5 x 34.5 cm; wood*

16. St. Sigismond and Sigismondo Pandolfo Malatesta, *1451; Rimini, Malatesta Temple, Reliquary Chapel; 257 x 345 cm; the fresco was detached and moved Signed and dated "PETRI DE BURGO OPUS MCCCCLI"*

17. St. Julian, *c. 1455; Sansepolcro, Museo Civico; 137 x 135 cm; the fresco was moved from the apse of the church of Sant'Agostino in Sansepolcro*

The Legend of the True Cross
Frescoes and mixed media on walls; 1452-66; Arezzo, church of San Francesco, choir chapel.
Commissioned by the Bacci family of Arezzo, the decoration of the chapel was begun in 1447
by the Florentine painter Bicci di Lorenzo, and on his death in 1452 Piero succeeded him.
With the assistance of helpers, the artist completed the vast and complex cycle over an extended period of time,
with intervals for trips to Rome in 1458-59 and while working at the same time on other projects.

18. The Legend of the True Cross: The Death of Adam; *390 x 747 cm; lunette on the right wall*

19. The Legend of the True Cross: The Adoration of the Sacred Wood and the Meeting of Solomon and the Queen of Sheba; *336 x 747 cm; middle register of the right wall*

20. The Legend of the True Cross: The Adoration of the Sacred Wood and the Meeting of Solomon and the Queen of Sheba; *detail*

21. The Legend of the True Cross: The Adoration of the Sacred Wood and the Meeting of Solomon and the Queen of Sheba; *detail*

22. The Legend of the True Cross: The Transportation of the Sacred Wood;
356 x 190 cm; middle register of the back wall, to the right

23. The Legend of the True Cross: The Dream of Constantine; *329 x 190 cm;*
lower register of the back wall, to the right

◀ 24. *Opposite:* The Legend of the True Cross: The Annunciation; *329 x 193 cm;*
lower register of the back wall, to the left
25. The Legend of the True Cross: The Annunciation; *detail*

◄ 26. *Opposite*: The Legend of the True Cross: The Torment of the Hebrew; *356 x 193 cm;*
middle register of the back wall, to the left
27. The Legend of the True Cross: The Torment of the Hebrew; *detail*

28. **The Legend of the True Cross: The Victory of Constantine over Maxentius**; *322 x 764 cm; lower register of the right wall*

29. The Legend of the True Cross: The Finding of the Three Crosses and the Verification of the True Cross; *356 x 747 cm; middle register of the left wall*

30. The Legend of the True Cross: The Finding of the Three Crosses and the Verification of the True Cross; *detail*
31. Opposite: The Legend of the True Cross: The Finding of the Three Crosses and the Verification of the True Cross; *detail* ▶

32. The Legend of the True Cross: The Battle of Heraclius and Cosroe; *329 x 742 cm; lower register of the left wall*

33. The Legend of the True Cross: The Battle of Heraclius and Cosroe; *detail*

34. The Legend of the True Cross: The Battle of Heraclius and Cosroe; *detail*

35. The Legend of the True Cross: The Battle of Heraclius and Cosroe; *detail*

36. The Legend of the True Cross: The Battle of Heraclius and Cosroe; *detail*

37. The Legend of the True Cross: The Exaltation of the Cross; *390 x 747 cm; lunette from the left wall*

38. The Legend of the True Cross: The Exaltation of the Cross; *detail*

39. The Legend of the True Cross: A Prophet; *base 193 cm; upper register of the back wall, to the left*

40. The Legend of the True Cross: A Prophet; *base 190 cm; upper register of the back wall, to the right*

41. Mary Magdalen, c. 1460; Arezzo, Cathedral; 190 x 80 cm; fresco

42. The Madonna del Parto ("Pregnant Madonna"), c. 1460; Monterchi (Arezzo), Cemetery Chapel; 260 x 203 cm; the fresco has been detached and moved in loco

43. The Madonna del Parto; *detail*

44. The Madonna del Parto; *detail*

45. The Resurrection of Christ, *1460-63; Sansepolcro, Museo Civico; 225 x 200 cm; fresco*

46. The Resurrection of Christ; *detail*

47. *Virgin and Child with Angels, 1465-70; Williamstown (Massachusetts), Sterling and Francine Clark Art Institute; 106 x 78 cm; wood*

48. Hercules, 1460-66; Boston, Isabella Stewart Gardner Museum; 151 x 126 cm; the fresco has been detached
This work is from the house in Sansepolcro that was the property of the family of Piero della Francesca.

Diptych of the Counts of Urbino
wooden panels; c. 1465; each 47 x 33 cm; Florence, Uffizi Gallery
From the ducal palace of Urbino; the original frame that joined the two portraits has been lost.
49. Diptych of the Counts of Urbino: Portrait of Battista Sforza; recto

50. Diptych of the Counts of Urbino: Portrait of Federigo II da Montefeltro; *recto*

CLARVS INSIGNI VEHITVR TRIVMPHO ·
QVEM PAREM SVMMIS DVCIBVS PERHENNIS ·
FAMA VIRTVTVM CELEBRAT DECENTER ·
SCEPTRA TENENTEM

51. Diptych of the Counts of Urbino: Triumph of Federigo II da Montefeltro; *verso*

QVE MODVM REBVS TENVIT SECVNDIS ·
CONIVGIS MAGNI DECORATA RERVM ·
LAVDE GESTARVM VOLITAT PER ORA ·
CVNCTA VIRORVM ᵔ

52. Diptych of the Counts of Urbino: Triumph of Battista Sforza; *verso*

The Polyptych of St. Augustine, *tempera and oil (?) on wood; 1454-69*
Commissioned in 1454 by Angiolo di Giovanni di Simone of Sansepolcro to fulfill the wishes of his deceased brother Simone and his sister-in-law
Giovanna, this was made for the major altar of the church of Sant'Agostino. The ideal reconstruction of the polyptych, dismembered and dispersed,
is the work of modern art critics: the central partition and several minor portions have been lost.
53. Polyptych of St. Augustine: St. Augustine; *Lisbon, Museo Nacional de Arte Antigua; 136 x 67 cm; left lateral partition*

54. Polyptych of St. Augustine: The Archangel St. Michael;
London, National Gallery; 133 x 59.5 cm; left lateral partition

55. Polyptych of St. Augustine: St. John the Evangelist;
New York, The Frick Collection;
134 x 62.2 cm; right lateral partition

56. Polyptych of St. Augustine: St. Nicholas of Tolentino;
Milan, Museo Poldi Pezzoli;
139.4 x 59.2 cm; right lateral partition

57. Polyptych of St. Anthony, 1465-70; Perugia, Galleria Nazionale dell'Umbria; 338 x 230 cm;
tempera on wood
Formerly in the convent of the Franciscan nuns of St. Anthony in Perugia,
the polyptych is probably the result of the assembly, undertaken by Piero himself (with assistants)
to fulfill the wishes of the buyers, of two works planned in different styles and times.

58. Polyptych of St. Anthony: The Annunciation; *122 x 194 cm; the cyma*

59. Polyptych of St. Anthony: Saints Anthony of Padua and John the Baptist;
124 x 62 cm; left lateral partitions

60. Polyptych of St. Anthony: Saints Francis of Assisi and Elizabeth;
124 x 64 cm; right lateral partitions

61. Virgin with Child, Saints, Angels, and Federigo II da Montefeltro, *1472-74; Milan,*
Pinacoteca di Brera; 248 x 170 cm; from the church of San Bernardino in Urbino

62. Virgin with Child, Saints, Angels, and Federigo II da Montefeltro; *detail*

63. Virgin with Child, Saints, Angels, and Federigo II da Montefeltro; *detail*

64. Virgin with Child, Saints, Angels, and Federigo II da Montefeltro; *detail*

65. The Nativity, *1472-74; London, National Gallery; 126 x 123 cm*

66. The Nativity; *detail*

67. The Nativity; detail

68. Madonna with Child and Angels, *1470-75; Urbino, Galleria Nazionale delle Marche; 61 x 53.5 cm;*
from the church of Santa Maria delle Grazie of Senigallia (and thus also known as the Madonna di Senigallia)

LIST OF PLATES

CHRONOLOGY

c. 1420: Piero is born in Borgo San Sepolcro to Benedetto de' Franceschi and Romana di Perino da Monterchi.

1439: Piero is recorded together with Domenico Veneziano in a payment for the frescoes (lost) in the choir of the church of Sant'Egidio in Florence.

1442: Piero is recorded in Borgo San Sepolcro as a member of the town council.

1445: Year of the commission for the *Polyptych of Mercy*.

1449-50: In Ferrara Piero paints frescoes (lost) in the Este castle and in the church of Sant'Agostino.

1450: Signature and date of the *St. Jerome* in Berlin.

1451: Signature and date of the Malatesta Temple frescoes in Rimini.

1452: Succeeds Bicci di Lorenzo in the fresco decoration of the choir of San Francesco in Arezzo.

1454: Commission for the *Polyptych of St. Augustine*.

1459: Piero receives a payment for the frescoes (lost) in a room of the Vatican palaces in Rome.

1460: Date of the written dedication (lost) of the fresco with St. Ludovic in the municipal palace of Borgo San Sepolcro.

1462: Piero's brother Marco receives the final payment for the *Polyptych of Mercy*.

1466: The Brotherhood of the Annunziata in Arezzo commissions Piero to make a banner with the Annunciation (lost).

1467: Piero holds public office in Borgo San Sepolcro.

1469: Piero is recorded in Urbino for a work (never done) for the Brotherhood of Corpus Domini. Payment for the *Polyptych of St. Augustine*.

1471: Piero is listed among those who failed to pay their taxes in the commune of Borgo San Sepolcro.

1474: Payment for the frescoes (lost) in the abbey of Sansepolcro.

1478: Piero is commissioned to make a fresco (lost) for the Brotherhood of Mercy (Misericordia) in Sansepolcro.

1479-80: Movement and restoration of the *Resurrection* in the Palazzo dei Conservatori in Borgo San Sepolcro.

1480-82: Piero is the head of the priors of the Brotherhood of San Bartolomeo in Borgo San Sepolcro.

1487: Piero has his will prepared by the notary Lionardo di ser Mario Fedeli.

1492: Piero dies in San Sepolcro and is buried in the abbey.

TOPOGRAPHICAL INDEX OF THE WORKS

AREZZO
Church of San Francesco: *The Legend of the True Cross*
Duomo: *St. Mary Magdalen*

BERLIN-DAHLEM
Gemäldegalerie: *The Penitent St. Jerome*

BOSTON
The Isabella Stewart Gardner Museum: *Hercules*

FLORENCE
Uffizi Gallery: *Diptych of the Counts of Urbino*

LISBON
Museu Nacional de Arte Antiga: *St. Augustine*

LONDON
National Gallery: *The Baptism of Christ; The Nativity; The Archangel St. Michael*

MILAN
Museo Poldi Pezzoli: *St. Nicholas of Tolentino*
Pinacoteca di Brera: *Virgin with Child, Saints, Angels, and Federigo II da Montefeltro*

MONTERCHI (Arezzo)
Cemetry Chapel: *La Madonna del Parto*

NEW YORK
The Frick Collection (in deposit at the Princeton Art Museum): *The Crucifixion*
The Frick Collection: *St. John the Evangelist (?); St. Monica; St. Augustine*

PARIS
Musée du Louvre: *Portrait of Sigismondo Pandolfo Malatesta*

PERUGIA
Galleria Nazionale dell'Umbria: *Polyptych of St. Anthony*

RIMINI
Malatesta Temple: *St. Sigismond and Sigismondo Pandolfo Malatesta*

ROME
Basilica of Santa Maria Maggiore: *St. Luke the Evangelist*

SANSEPOLCRO (Arezzo)
Museo Civico: *Polyptych of Mercy; The Resurrection of Christ; St. Julian; St. Ludovic*

URBINO
Galleria Nazionale delle Marche: *The Flagellation of Christ; Madonna with Child and Angels*

VENICE
Galleria dell'Accademia: *St. Jerome and a Devout*

WASHINGTON, D.C.
National Gallery of Art: *St. Apollonia*

WILLIAMSTOWN (Massachusetts)
Sterling and Francine Clark Art Institute: *Virgin and Child with Angels*

ESSENTIAL BIBLIOGRAPHY

Alberti, L.B. *Della pittura*, 1436. Edited by L. Malle, Florence, 1950.

Alpatov, M. "Les fresques de Piero della Francesca à Arezzo. Sémantique et stilistique," in *Commentari*, XIV, 1, 1963.

Barolsky, P. "Piero's Native Wit," in *Source*, 1982.

Berenson, B. *Central Italian Painters*, London, 1897 (ed. 1909; 1911).

—. *Italian Painters of the Renaissance*, London, 1954.

—. *Italian Pictures of the Renaissance*, Oxford, 1932 (ed. 1953).

—. *Piero della Francesca or: the Ineloquent in Art*, London, 1954.

Borgo, L. "New Questions for Piero's Flagellation," in *The Burlington Magazine*, 121, 1979.

Brisson, D.W. "Piero della Francesca's Egg Again," in *The Art Bulletin*, 62, 1980.

Clark, K. *Piero della Francesca*, London-New York, 1951.

—. "Piero della Francesca's Augustin Altarpiece," in *The Burlington Magazine*, LXXXIX, 1947.

Clough, C.H. "Federigo de Montefeltro's Patronage of the Arts, 1468-1482" in *Journal of the Warburg and Courtauld Institutes*, 36, 1973.

—. "Piero della Francesca. Some Problems of His Art and Chronology," in *Apollo*, 91, 1970.

Cocke, R. "Piero della Francesca and the Development of Italian Landscape Painting," in *The Burlington Magazine*, 122, 1980.

Crowe, J.A., and Cavalcaselle, G.B. *A History of Painting in Italy from the Second to the Sixteenth Century*, London, 1864-66.

Davies, E.M., and Snyder, D. "Piero della Francesca's Madonna of Urbino," in *Gazette des Beaux-Arts*, 75, 1970.

Davies, M. *National Gallery Catalogues. The Earlier Italian Schools*, London, 1951, 1961.

Davis, M.D. *Piero della Francesca: A Study of His Trattato d'Abaco and Libellus de Quinque Corporibus Regolaribus*, Ravenna, 1977.

De Tolnay, C. "Conceptions religieuses dans la peinture de Piero della Francesca," in *Arte Antica e Moderna*, 23, 1963.

Edgerton, Y. *The Renaissance Discovery of Linear Perspective*, New York, 1975.

Egmond, W. van, "A Second Manuscript of Piero della Francesca's Trattato d'Abaco," in *Manuscripta*, 1980.

Emmer, M. "Art and Mathematics: The Platonic Solids," in *Leonardo*, 15, 1982.

Focillon, H. *Piero della Francesca*, Paris, 1934-35 (published 1952).

Fredericksen, B.B., and Zeri, F. *Census of Pre-Nineteenth Century Italian Paintings in North American Public Collections*, Cambridge, 1972.

Gilbert, C. "Blind Cupid," in *Journal of the Warburg and Courtauld Institutes*, XXXII, 1970.

—. *Change in Piero della Francesca*, New York, 1968.

—. "New Evidence for the Date of Piero della Francesca's Count and Countess of Urbino," in *Marsyas*, I, 1941.

—. "Piero della Francesca's Flagellation: The Figures in the Foreground," in *The Art Bulletin*, 53, 1971.

Godby, M. "Letter on Piero's Annunciation in Relation to Aretine Painting," in *The Art Bulletin*, 58, 1976.

Goldner, C. "Note on the Iconography of Piero della Francesca's Annunciation in Arezzo," in *The Art Bulletin*, 56, 1974.

Gombrich, E.H. "The Repentance of Judas in Piero della Francesca's Flagellation of Christ," in *Journal of the Warburg and Courtauld Institutes*, XXII, 1959.

Graber, H. *Piero della Francesca*, Basel, 1920.

Guillaud, J. and M. *Piero della Francesca Poet of Form. The Frescoes of San Francesco di Arezzo*, Paris-New York, 1988.

Hendy, P. *Piero della Francesca and the Early Renaissance*, London, 1968.

Heydenreich, L.H. "Federico da Montefeltro, Building Patron. Some Remarks on the Ducal Palace at Urbino," in *Studien zur Architektur der Renaissance*, 1981.

Hoffman, J. "Piero della Francesca's Flagellation: A Reading from Jewish History," in *Zeitschrift für Kunstgeschichte*, XLIV, 1981.

Homolka, L. "Piero's Egg," in *The Art Bulletin*, 1982.

Jayawardene, S.A. "The Trattato d'Abaco and Libellus de Quinque Corporibus Regularibus," in *Aspects of the Italian Renaissance*, (Festschrift P.O. Kristeller), 1976.

Lavin, M. Aromberg. "The Altar of Corpus Domini in Urbino: Paolo Uccello, Joos van Ghent, Piero della Francesca," in *The Art Bulletin*, 49, 1967.

—. "The Antique Source for the Tempio Malatestiano's Greek Inscription," in *The Art Bulletin*, 59, 1977.

—. *Piero della Francesca. The Flagellation*, London, 1972.

—. *Piero della Francesca's Baptism of Christ*, New Haven - London, 1981.

—. "Piero della Francesca's Flagellation: The Triumph of Christian Glory," in *The Art Bulletin*, 50, 1968.

—. "Piero della Francesca's Fresco of Sigismondo Pandolfo Malatesta before St. Sigismond," in *The Art Bulletin*, 56, 1974.

—. "Piero della Francesca's Montefeltro Altarpiece: A Pledge of Fidelity," in *The Art Bulletin*, 51, 1969.

—. *Studies in Urbinate Painting. 1458-1474: Piero della Francesca, Paolo Uccello and Joos Van Ghent*, New York University (dissertation), 1973-74.

Laclotte, M. "Le portrait de Sigismond Malatesta par Piero della Francesca," in *Revue de l'Art*, 1978.

Lindekens, R. "Analyse sémiotique d'une fresque de Piero della Francesca: La Légende de la Vraie Croix," in *Journal Canadien de recherche sémiotique*, IV/3, 1976.

Longhi, R. "Piero dei Franceschi e lo sviluppo della pittura veneziana," in *L'Arte*, 1913.

—. *Piero della Francesca*, Rome, 1927: reprinted in Longhi, R., *Opere complete* (with additions up to 1962), vol. III, Florence, 1963.

—. *Piero della Francesca. La leggenda della Croce*, Milan, 1951, 1955.

Marinesco, C. "Echos byzantins dans l'oeuvre de Piero della Francesca," in *Bulletin de la Société Nationale des Antiquaires de France*, 1958.

Meiss, M. "Addendum Ovologicum," in *The Art Bulletin*, XXXVI, 1954.

—. "A Documented Altarpiece by Piero della Francesca,"

in *The Art Bulletin*, XXIII, 1941.

—. *The Great Age of Fresco. Discoveries and Survivals*, The Metropolitan Museum of Art, New York, 1970.

—. "Not an Ostrich Egg?" in *The Art Bulletin*, 1975.

—. "Once again Piero della Francesca's Montefeltro Altarpiece," in *The Art Bulletin*, XLVIII, 1966.

—. "Ovum Struthionis, Symbol and Allusion in Piero della Francesca's Montefeltro Altarpiece," in *Studies in Art and Literature for Belle da Costa Greene*, Princeton, 1954.

Muratova, X. "Piero della Francesca for the Louvre," in *The Burlington Magazine*, 120, 1978.

Naumann, F.M. "New Light on Some Old Perspective Problems and Piero's Egg for the Dozenth Time," in *Iris, Notes on the History of Art*, I, 1982.

Oertel, R. "Petri de Burgo Opus," in *Studies in late Medieval Painting in honor of Millard Meiss* (I vol.), New York, 1977.

Paolucci, A. *Piero della Francesca*, Florence, 1989.

—. *Piero della Francesca. Catalogo completo*, Florence, 1990.

Peterson, T. Gouman. "Piero della Francesca's Flagellation: An Historical Interpretation," in *Storia dell'Arte*, 28, 1976.

Podro, M. *Piero della Francesca's Legend of the True Cross*, University of Newcastle upon Tyne, Newcastle upon Tyne, 1974.

Poseq, A.W.G. "Ambiguities of Perspective in the Murals of Piero della Francesca," in *Assaph, Studies in Art History*, 1, 1980.

Ragusa, I. "Egg Reopened," in *The Art Bulletin*, 53, 1971.

Ricci, C. *Piero della Francesca*, Rome, 1910.

Rzepinska, M. "The Peculiar Greyhounds of Sigismondo Malatesta. An Attempt to Interpret the Fresco of Piero della Francesca in Rimini," in *L'Arte*, 13, 1971.

—. "Reply with Rejoinder to M.A. Lavin's Piero della Francesca's Fresco of Sigismondo Pandolfo Malatesta before St. Sigismond," in *The Art Bulletin*, 57, 1975.

Santi. G. *Cronica rimata. 1490-95*, edited by H. Holtwinger, Stuttgart, 1893.

Schmidt, D. *Piero della Francesca*, Leipzig, 1970.

Schneider, L. "The Iconography of Piero della Francesca's Frescoes Illustrating the Legend of the True Cross in the Church of San Francesco in Arezzo," in *The Art Quarterly*, 21, 1969.

Shearman, J. "The Logic and Realism of Piero della Francesca," in *Festschrift Ulrich Middeldorf*, Berlin, 1968.

Smirnov, N. "Piero della Francesca," in *Hudoznik*, I, 1973.

Tanner, M. "Concordia in Piero della Francesca's Baptism of Christ," in *The Art Quarterly*, 35, 1972.

Van Marle, R. *The Development of the Italian Schools of Painting*, XI, The Hague, 1929.

Vasari, G. *Lives of the Artists* (1550 and 1568). English trans. by Gaston de Vere, 1912-14.

Venturi, A. *Storia dell'Arte italiana*, VII, 1, Milan, 1911.

Venturi, L. *Piero della Francesca*, Geneva, 1954.

Waters, W.G. *Piero della Francesca*, London, 1901.

Welliver, W. "The Flagellation of Christ and the Brother of the Duke of Urbino and Two Councilors," in *Gazette des Beaux-Arts*, 81, 1973.

—. "Symbolic Architecture of Domenico Veneziano and Piero della Francesca," in *The Art Quarterly*, 36, 1973.

—. "The Visit of the Queen of Sheba to King Solomon, in *Connaissance Arts*, 252, 1973.

Wittkower, R., and Carter, B.A.R. "The Perspective of Piero della Francesca's Flagellation," in *Journal of the Warburg and Courtauld Institutes*, 16, 1953.

Wohl, H. "In Detail: Piero della Francesca's Resurrection Fresco," in *Portfolio*, 2, 1981.

For the color illustrations, thanks are due the museums and public and private collections cited in the captions as well as the Archivio Fotografico Scala (Florence). For the black-and-white illustrations: Archivio Fotografico Scala (Florence).

Printed in February 1991
by Amilcare Pizzi S.p.A., Cinisello Balsamo (Milan), Italy